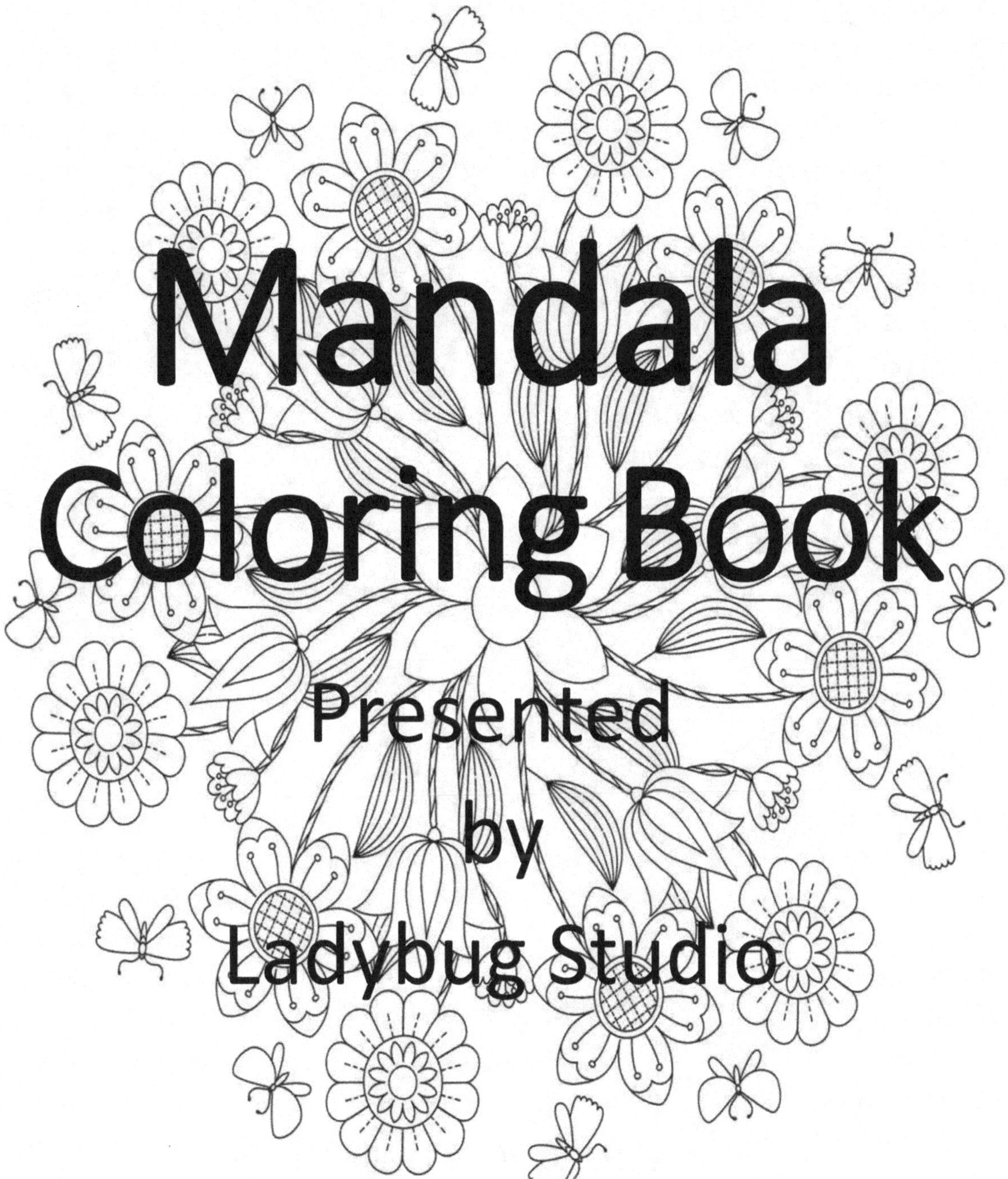

Mandala Coloring Book

Presented

by

Ladybug Studio

Ladybug Studio

Test your colors here

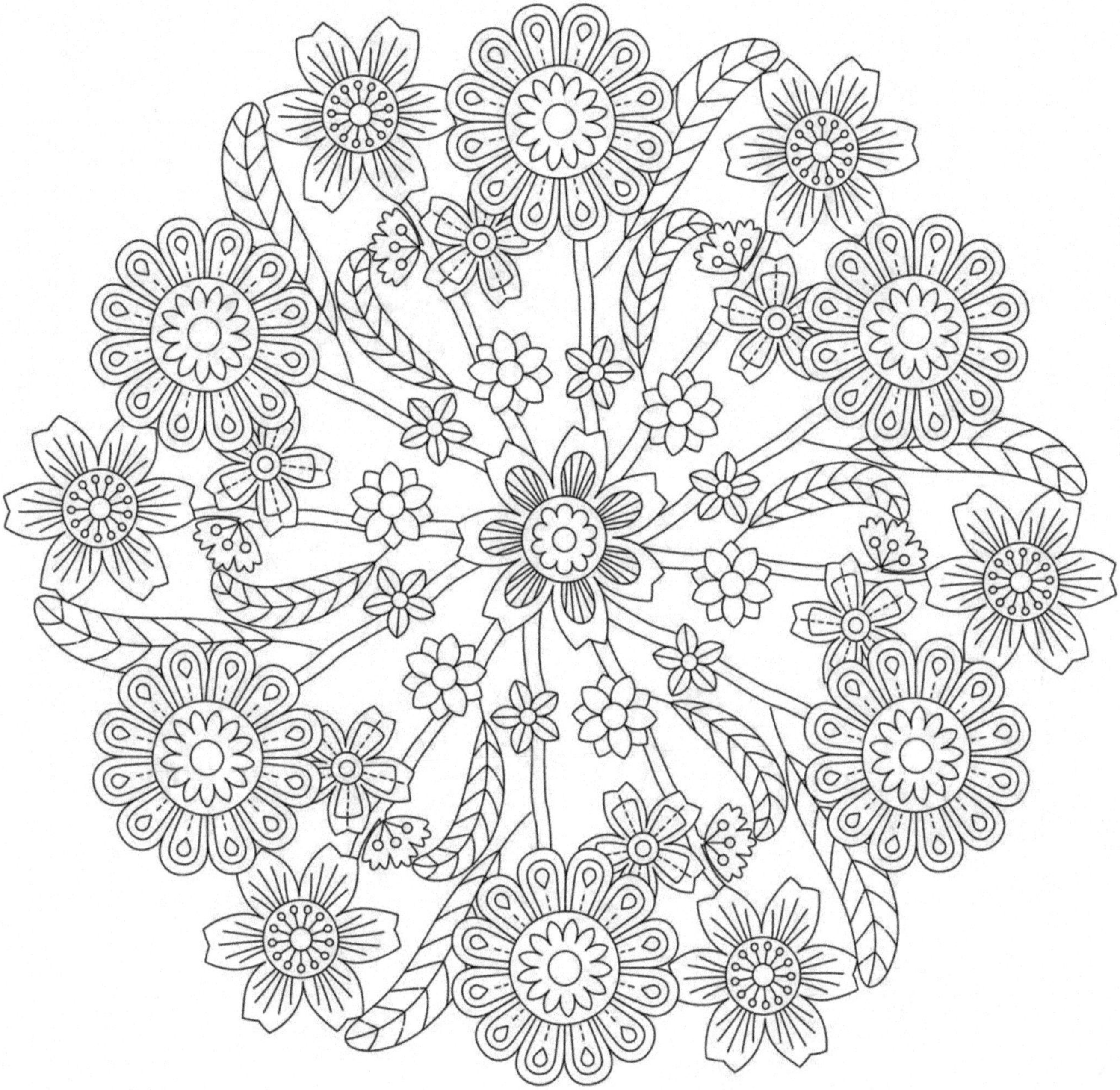

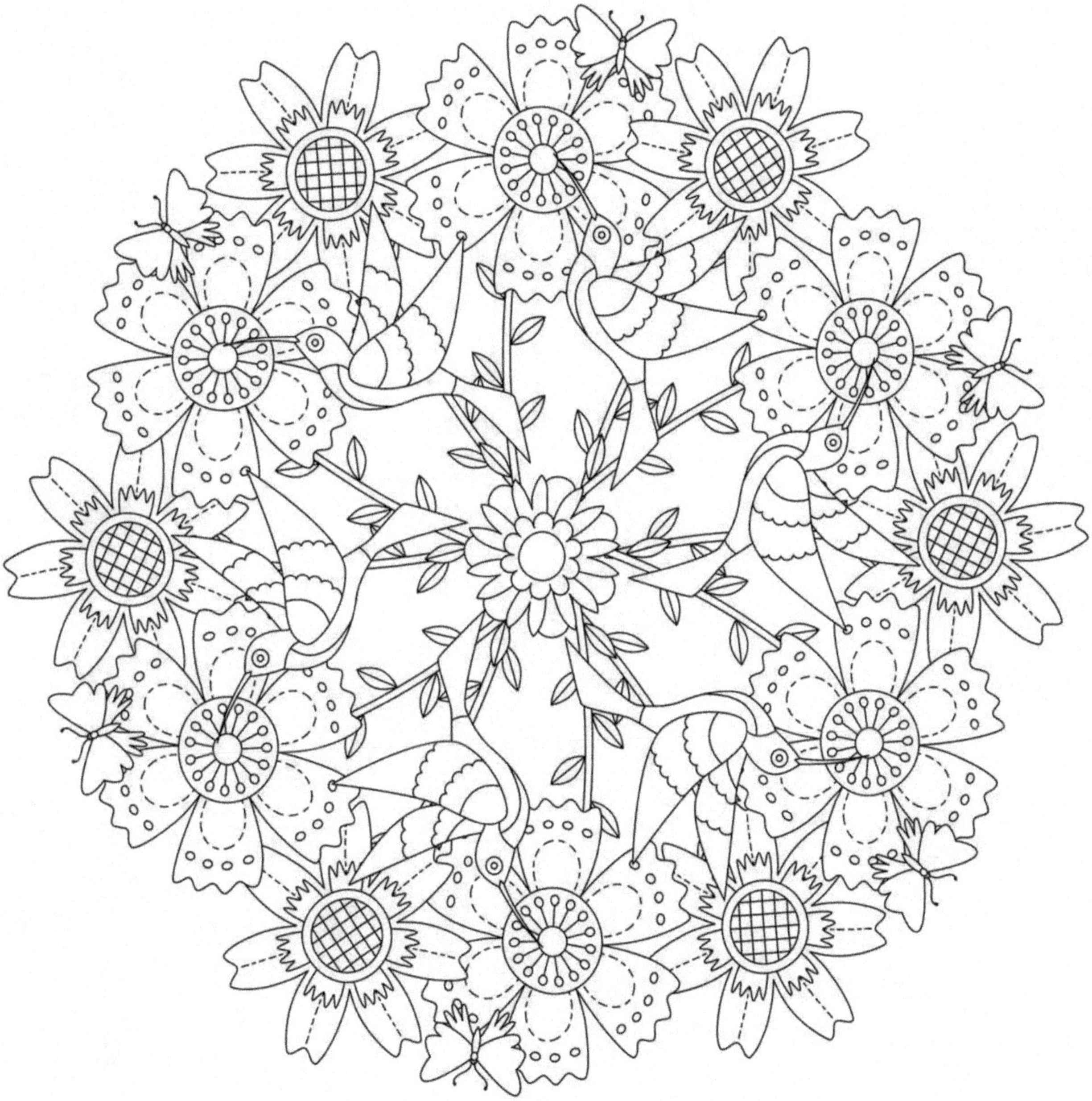

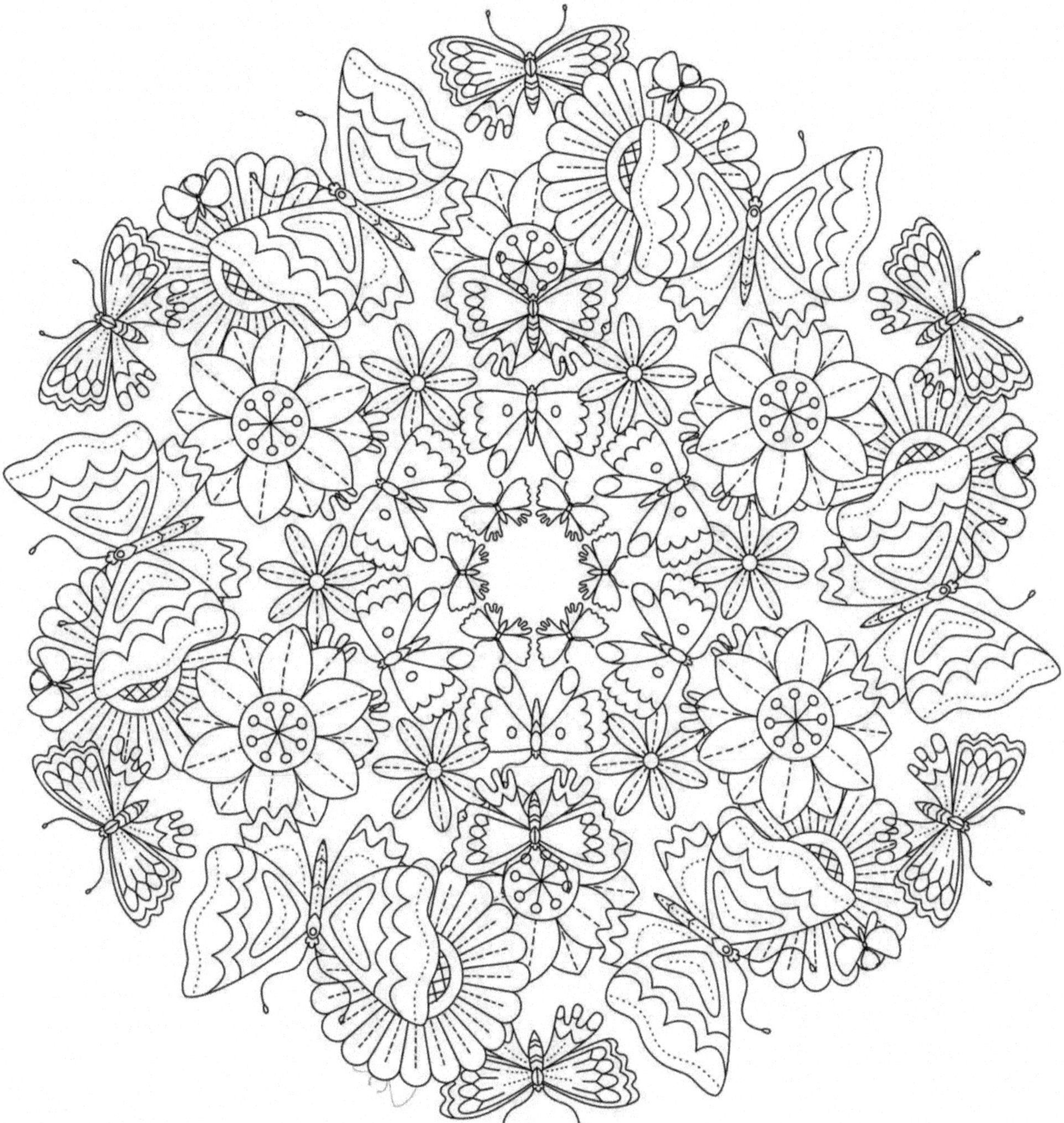

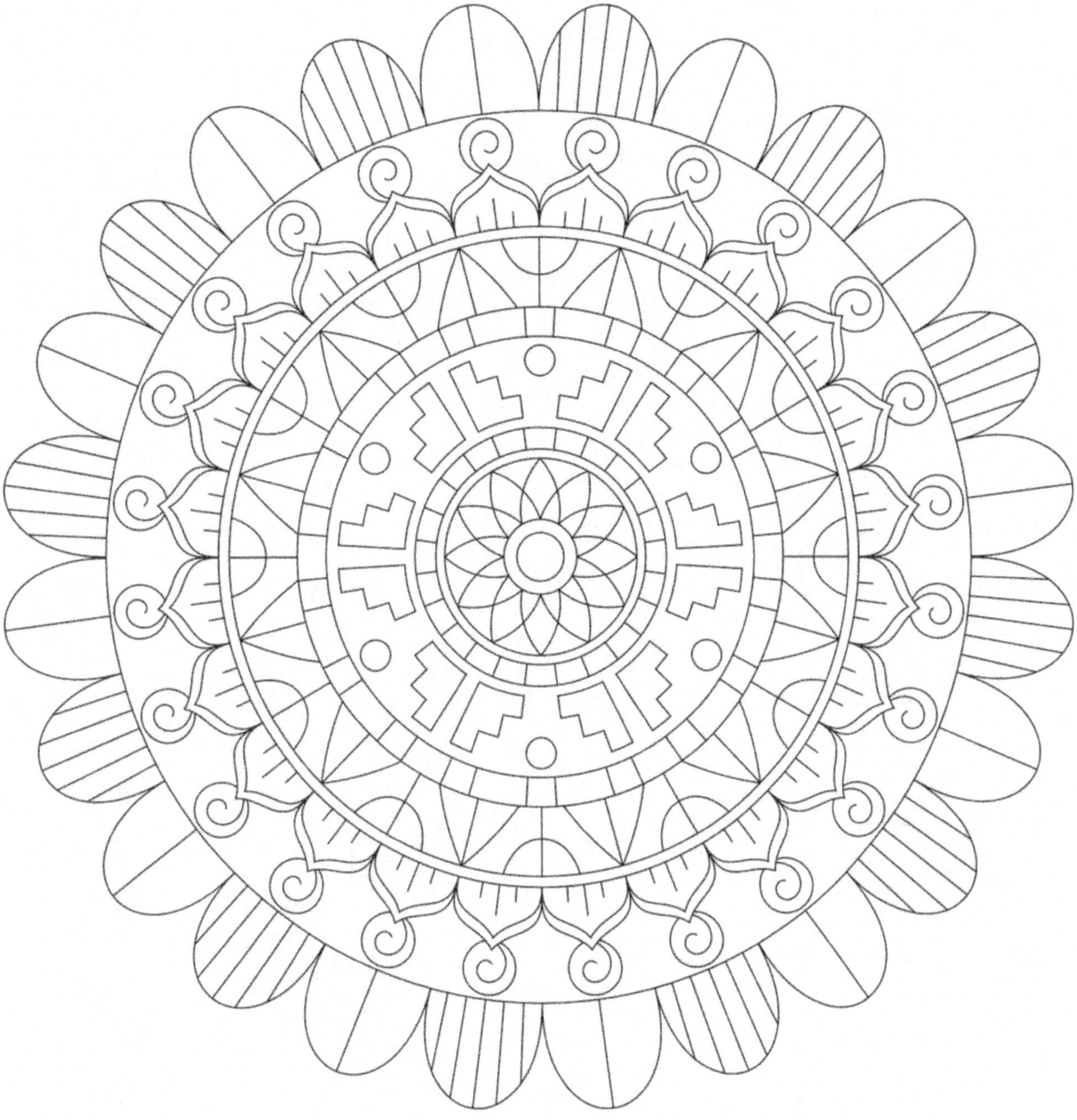

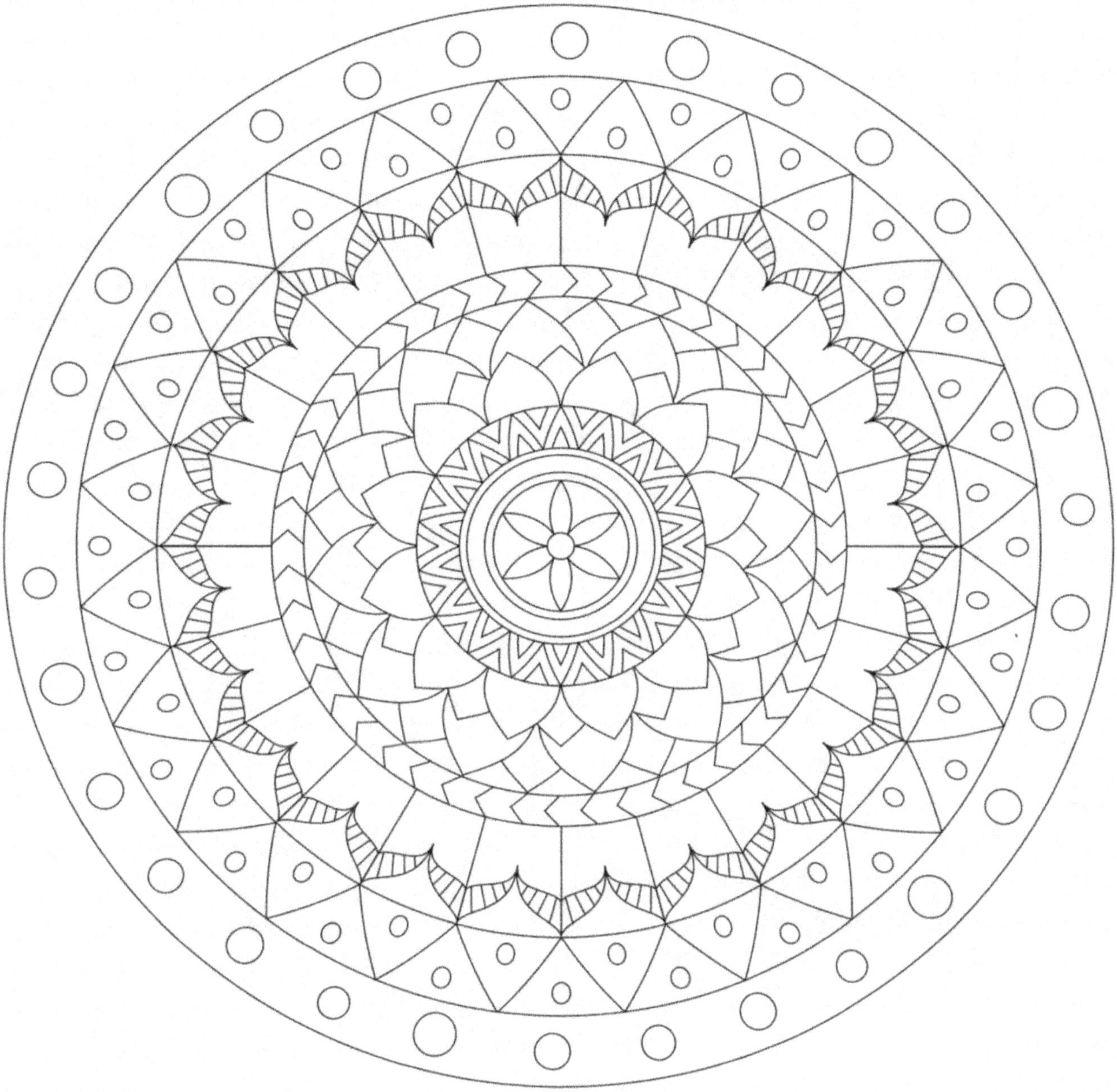

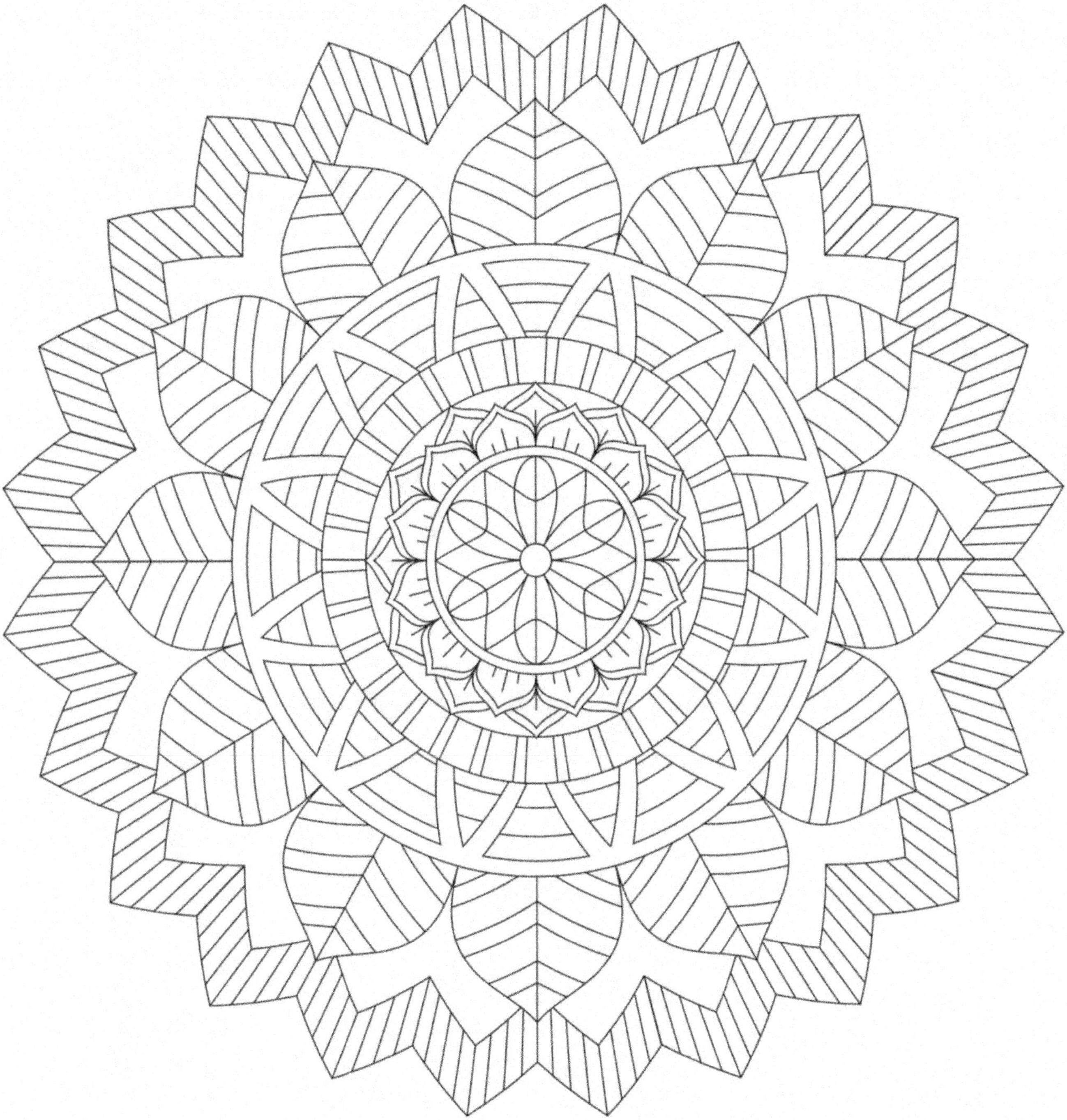

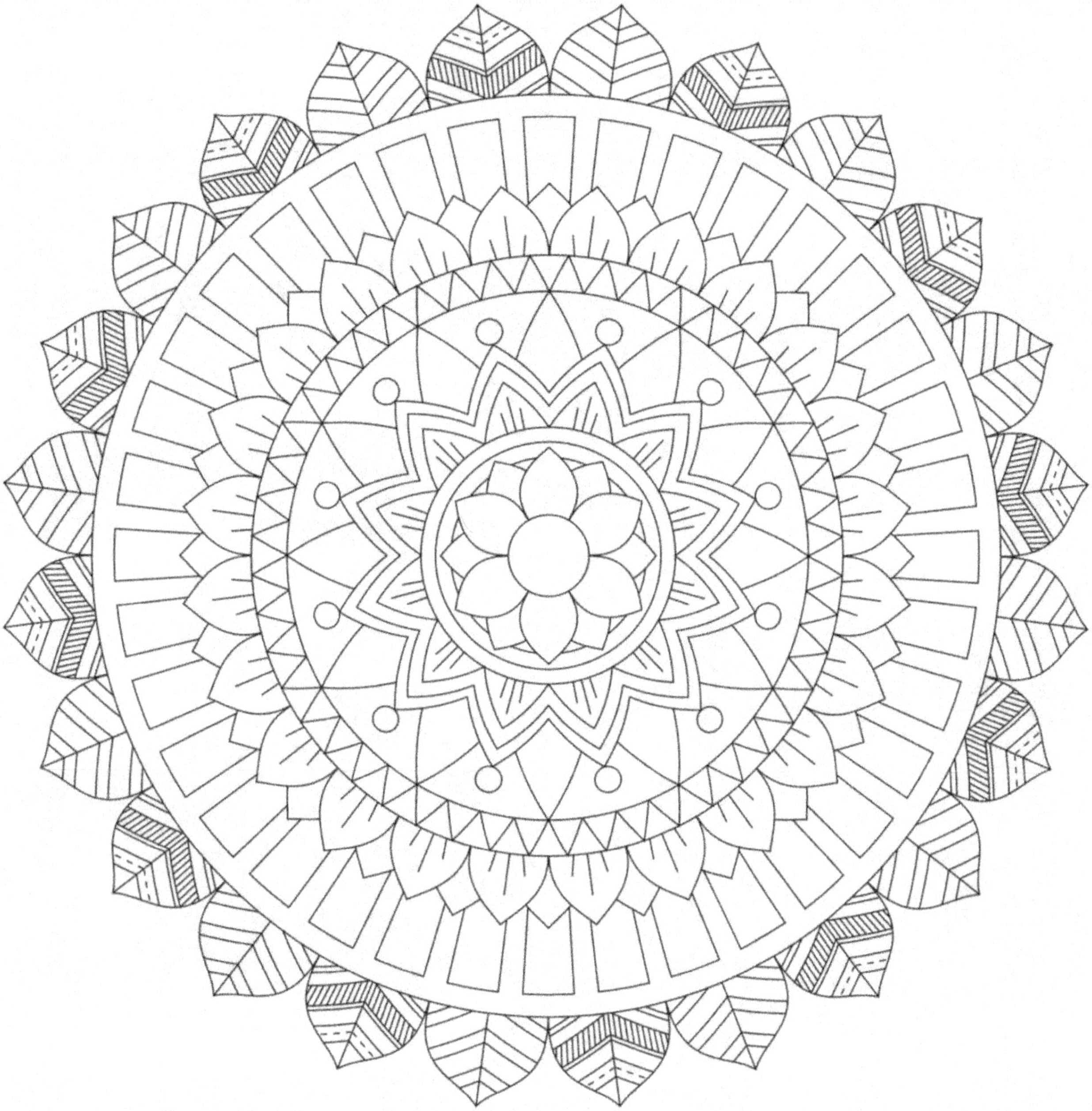

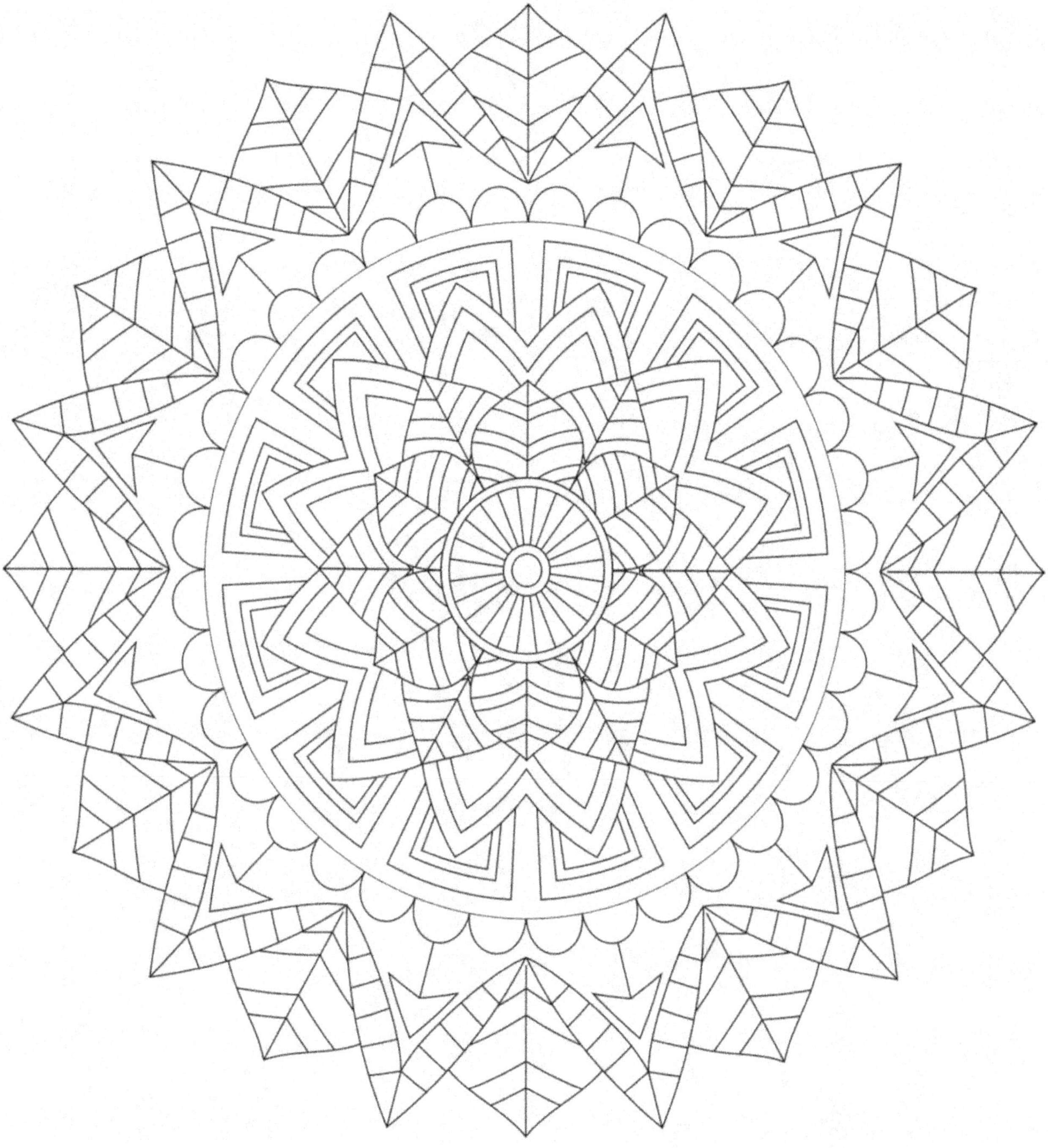

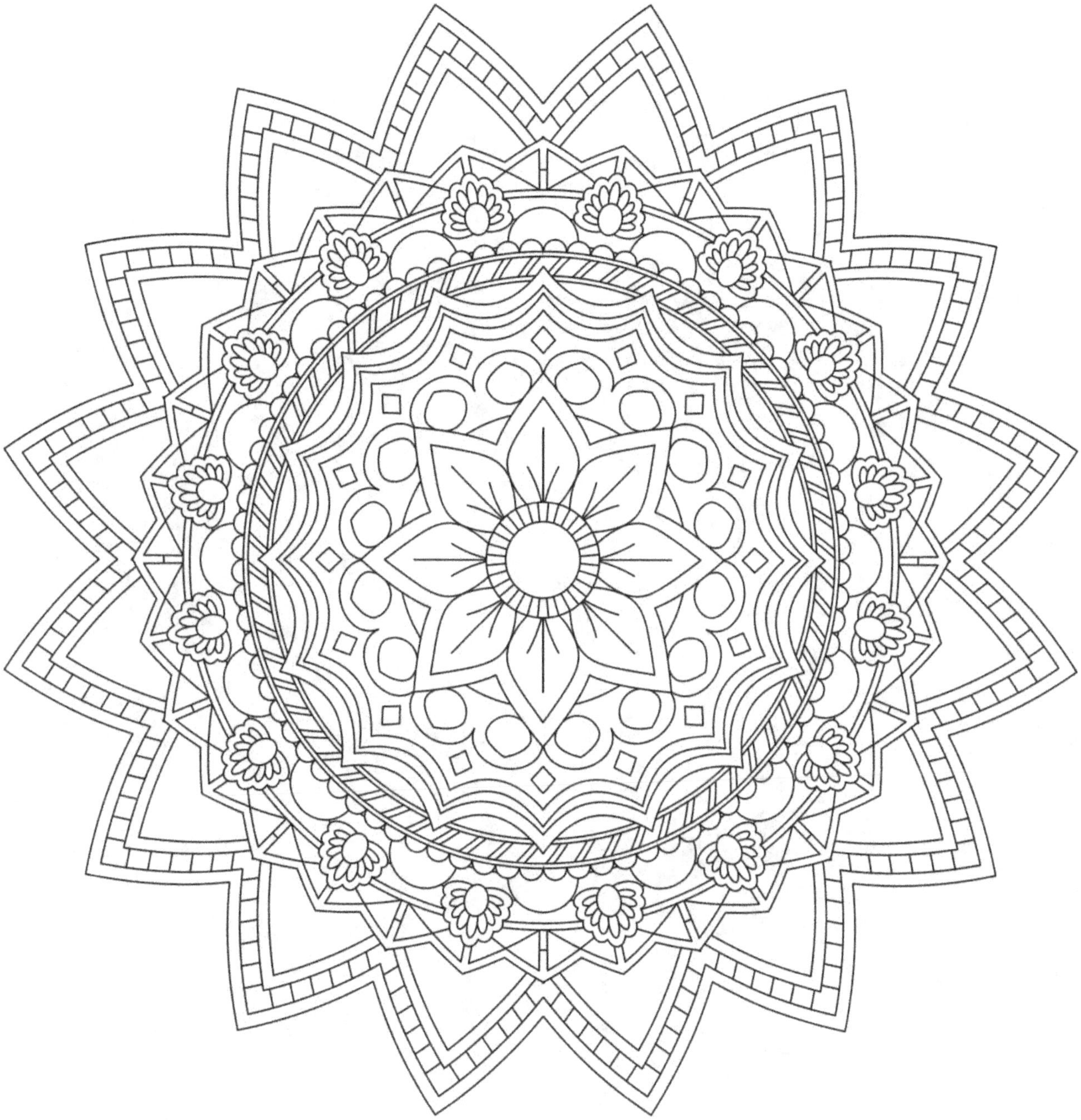

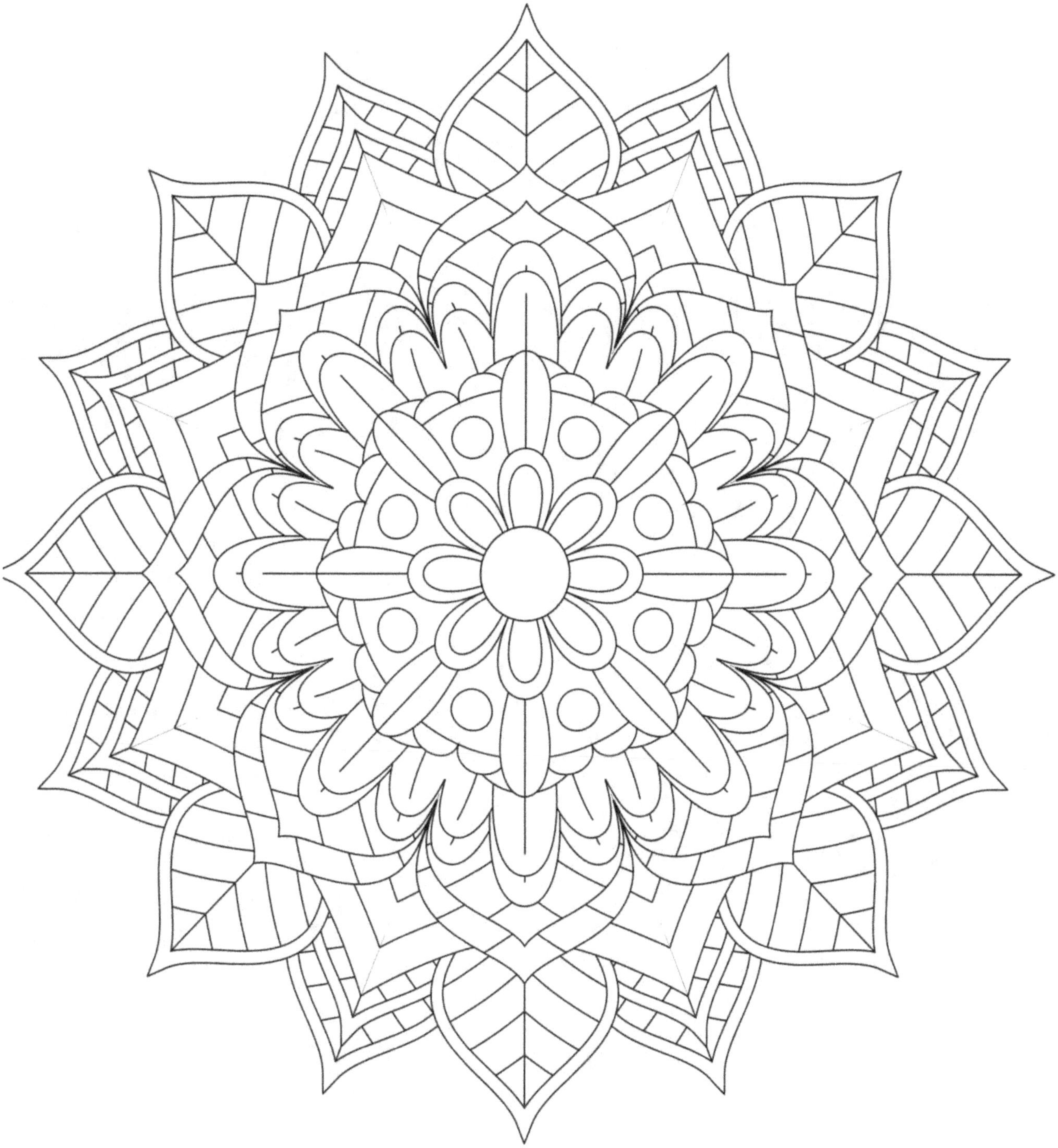

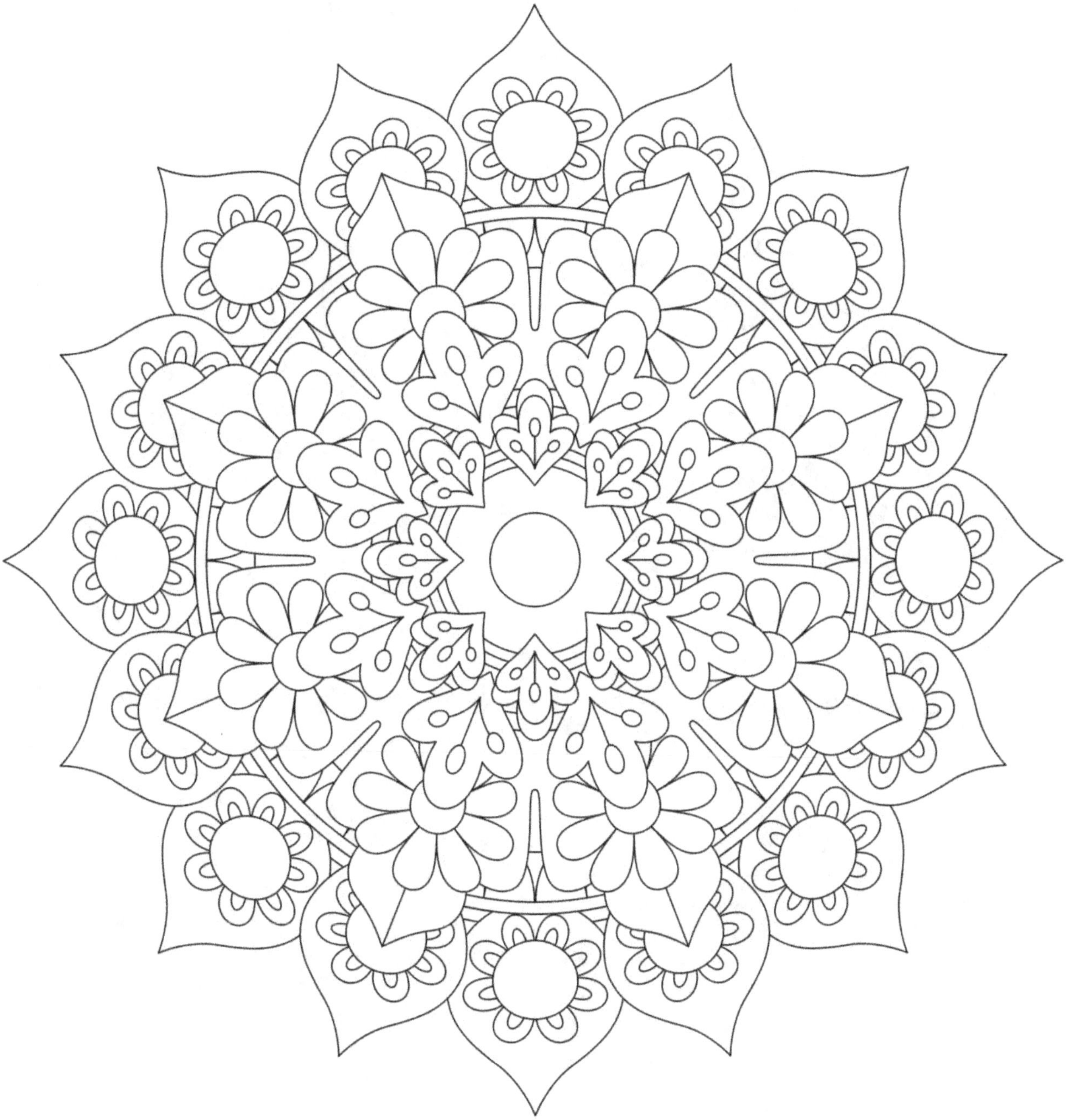

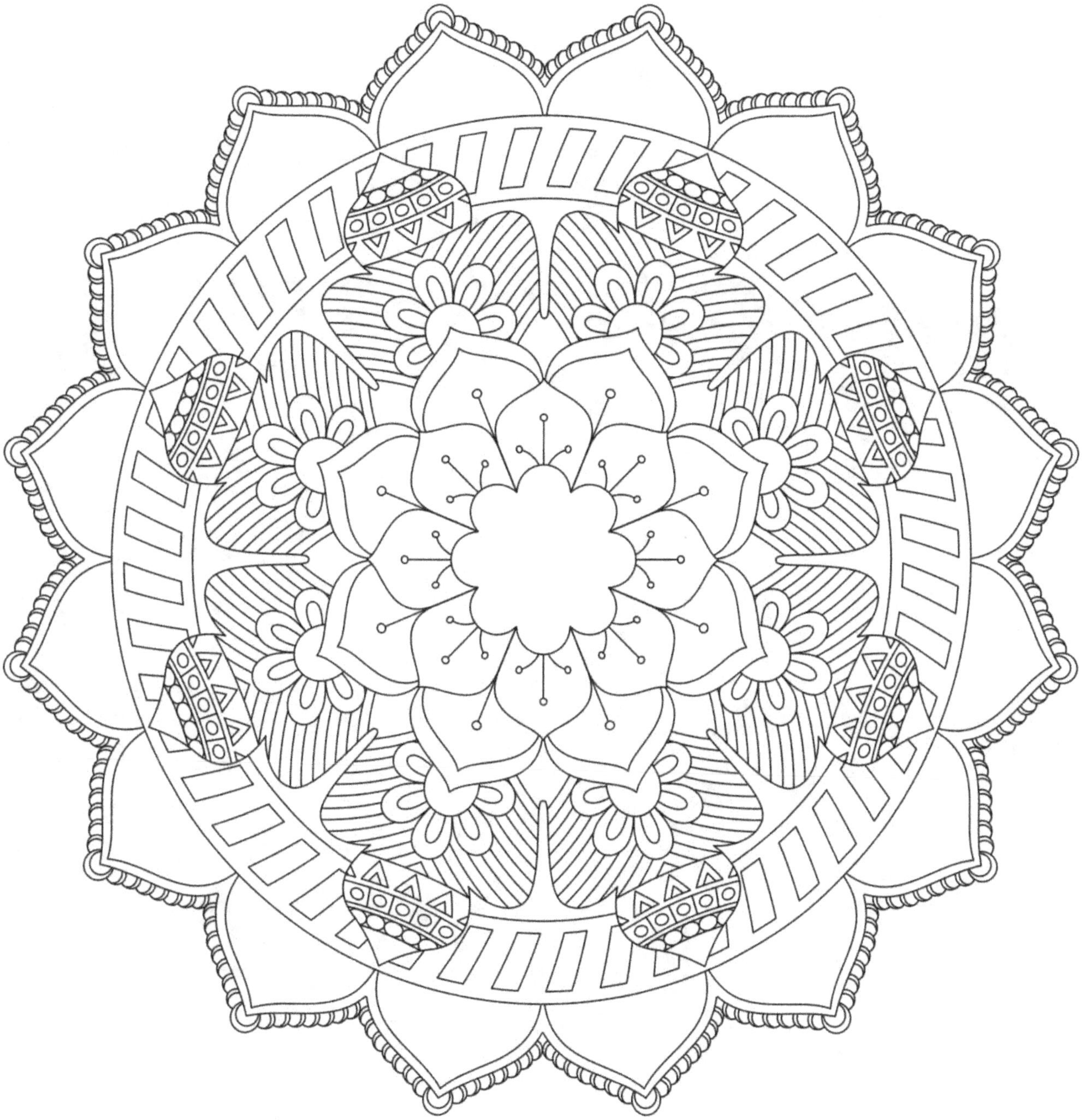

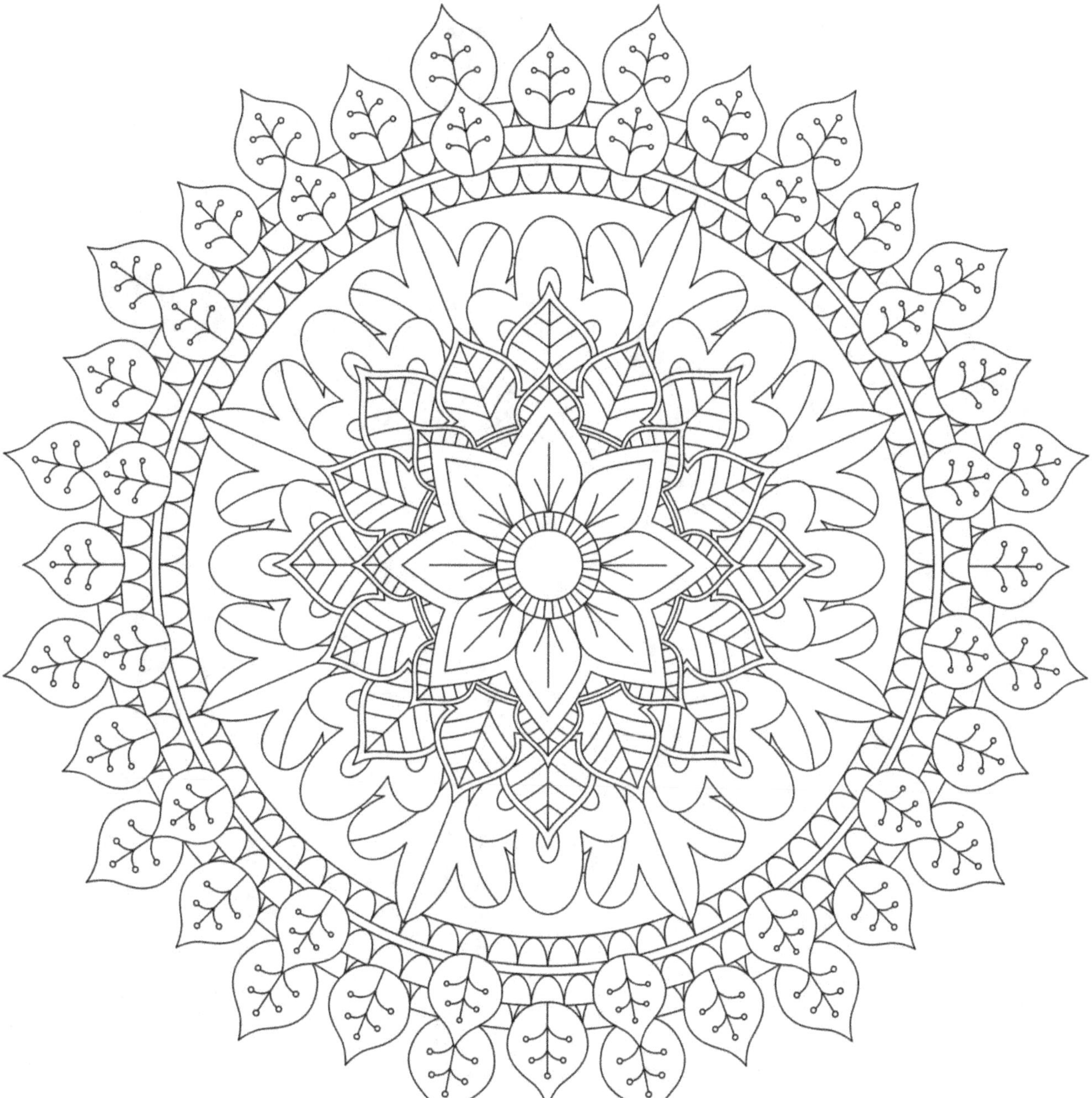

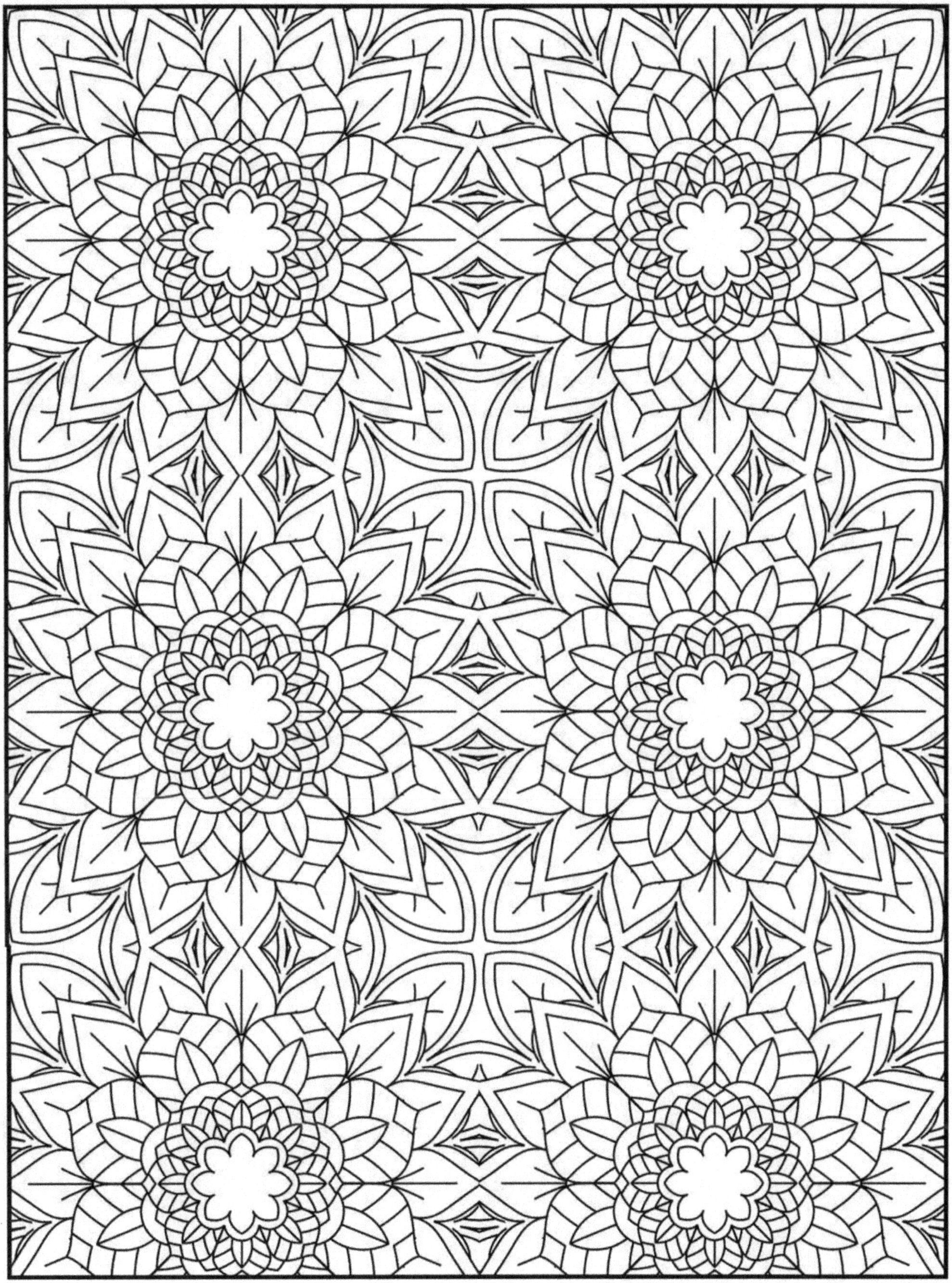

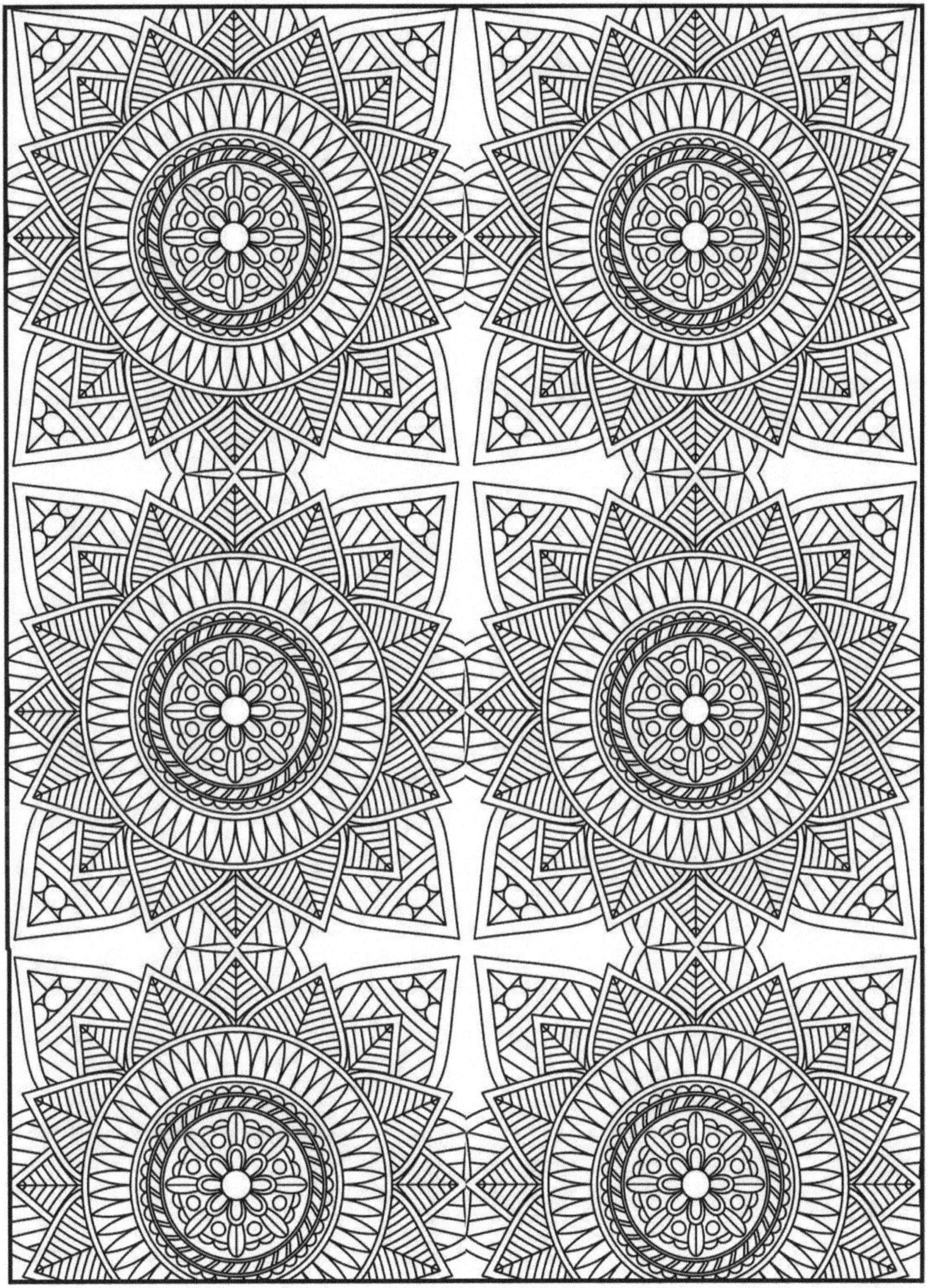

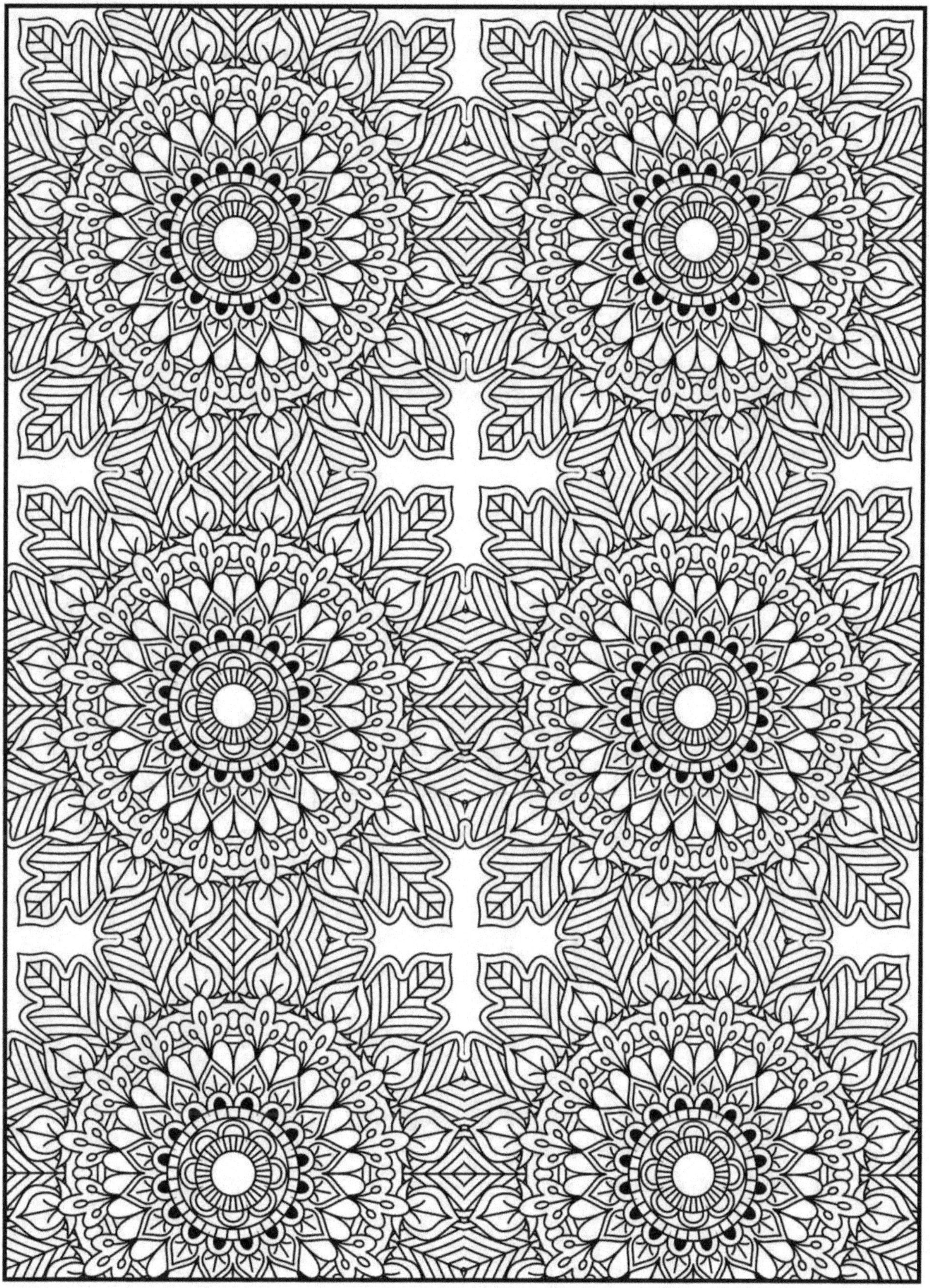

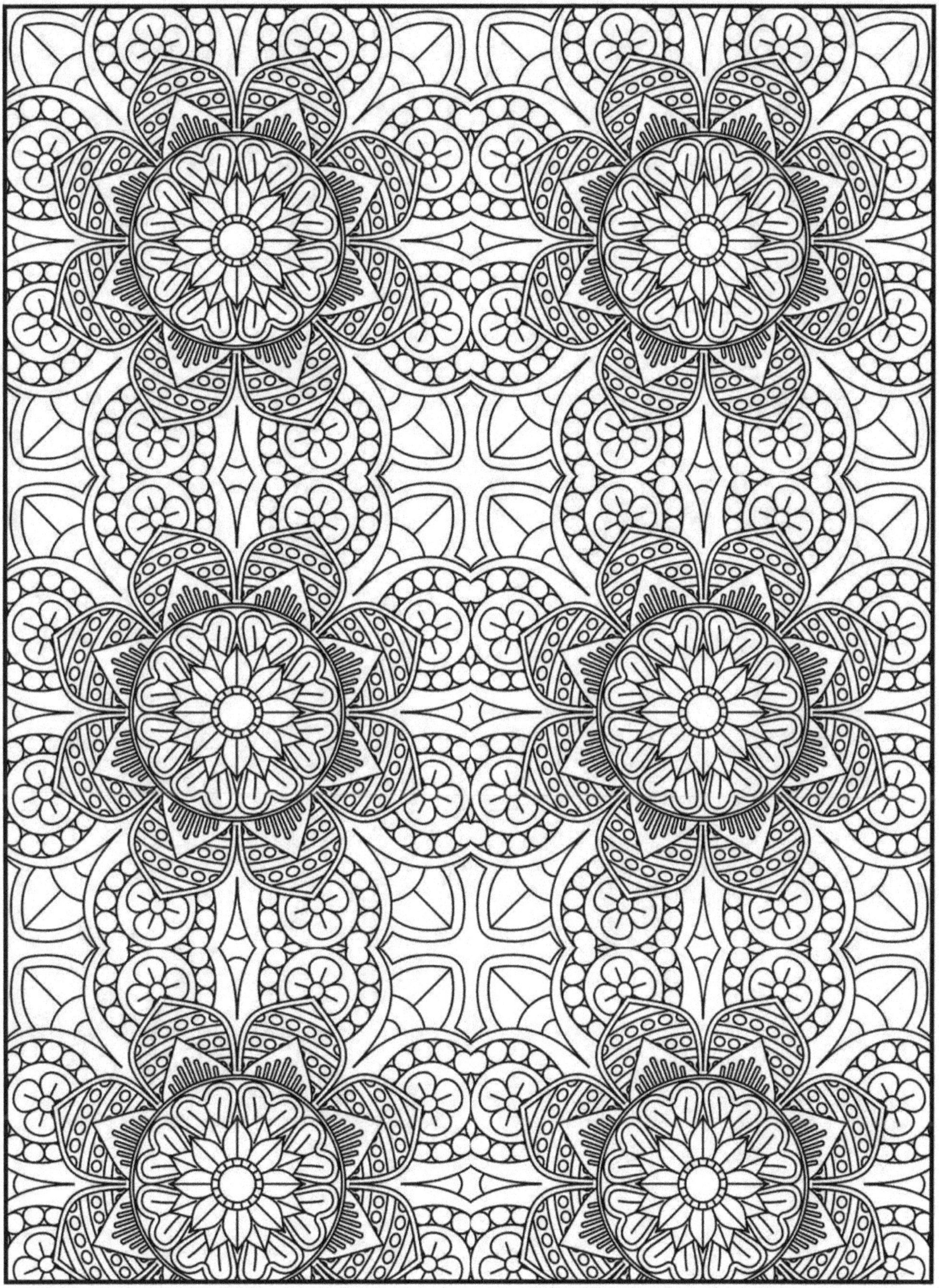

www.ingramcontent.com/pod-product-compliance
Lightning Source LLC
Chambersburg PA
CBHW080628220526
45467CB00011B/3420
* 9 7 8 1 7 0 5 3 3 0 2 7 2 *